10830965

MD in the Black

A Personal Finance Primer
for Medical Residents

MD in the Black

A Personal Finance Primer
for Medical Residents

First Edition

Editor-in-Chief

Eric Shappell, MD, MHPE

Editors

James Ahn, MD, MHPE
Ryan McKillip, MD

Copyright © 2018 by EM Fundamentals

All rights reserved. No part of this book may be reproduced, stored in a retrieval system, or transmitted in any form, or by any means, electronic, mechanical, photocopying, recording, or otherwise, without the express written consent of the publisher, except in the case of brief excerpts in either articles or reviews where a citation of the source is included.

EM Fundamentals is a registered trademark of EM Fundamentals, LLC.

www.MDintheBlack.com

www.EMFundamentals.com

ISBN: 9781726712958

Cover design by Mary Kate Venturini.
Printed in the United States of America.

Disclaimer
We (the authors, editors, and publisher) are not financial professionals. While we have used our best efforts, we make no claims to the accuracy or completeness of the contents of this book. Content including strategies and examples described in this book may not be appropriate for your situation. This content should not be considered financial, legal, accounting, or other professional advice. If you have any financial, legal, accounting, or other questions, you should consult a licensed professional in your state. Neither the authors, the editors, nor the publisher shall be liable for any damages resulting from actions taken related to the content of this book.

Contributors

Editor-in-Chief

Eric Shappell, MD, MHPE
Assistant Director, BWH/MGH HAEMR
Assistant Director, Emergency Medicine Clerkship
Massachusetts General Hospital
Harvard Medical School
Boston, MA

Editors

James Ahn, MD, MHPE
Associate Director, Emergency Medicine Residency
Director, Medical Education Fellowship
University of Chicago
Chicago, IL

Ryan McKillip, MD
Resident Physician
Advocate Christ Medical Center
Oak Lawn, IL

Authors

Michael Ernst, MD
Attending Physician
Emergency Medicine Consultants
Dallas, TX

Matthew Pirotte, MD
Assistant Director, Emergency Medicine Residency
Northwestern University
Chicago, IL

Eric Shappell, MD, MHPE
Assistant Director, BWH/MGH HAEMR
Assistant Director, Emergency Medicine Clerkship
Massachusetts General Hospital
Harvard Medical School
Boston, MA

Sponsored by

Council of Residency Directors
in Emergency Medicine

www.cordem.org

Table of Contents

Preface

MD in the Black is an organization of medical educators striving to improve personal finance education for residents. Beginning as a thesis project, this initiative has grown to include multiple research papers,[1,2] a website,[3] a curriculum for graduate medical education training programs that is being used in multiple specialties around the country,[4] and this book.

Our mission is to empower residents to make informed financial decisions while in training. In addition to each of the contributors to this book, we would especially like to acknowledge other educators whose input and guidance has helped bring this project to fruition: Ara Tekian, PhD, MHPE,

---

[1] Shappell et al., *Personal Finance Education for Residents: A Qualitative Study of Resident Perspectives.* AEM Educ Train. 2018;2(3):195-203.
[2] McKillip et al., *Toward a Resident Personal Finance Curriculum: Quantifying Resident Financial Circumstances, Needs, and Interests.* Cureus. 2018;10(4):e2540.
[3] *MD in the Black.* Retrieved from https://www.MDintheBlack.com
[4] *MD in the Black: Resources.* Retrieved from https://www.MDintheBlack.com/resources

Yoon Soo Park, PhD, Ilene Harris, PhD, Mohammed Minhaj, MD, MBA, Aalok Kacha, MD, PhD, and James Woodruff, MD.

What does *MD in the Black* mean?

"In the black" is a financial idiom meaning "making a profit." This is in contrast to "in the red," which means operating at a loss. For most trainees, the transition from medical school to residency marks an important switch from years of operating "in the red" (due to education debt) to collecting a salary that hopefully puts them "in the black." Helping residents handle this transition is the focus of our efforts; therefore, this transition is reflected in our name: *MD in the Black*.

While doctors of medicine (MDs) are mentioned in our name, the information contained in this book is relevant to many other groups of medical trainees, including doctors of osteopathic medicine (DOs), dentists, and pharmacists. Similarly, while we hope that physicians in training read this book to learn this content as a medical student or during residency, this information is also applicable to fellows.

Introduction

As medical trainees enter residency and begin collecting a salary, several important financial decisions must be made. While seemingly limitless financial advice can be found in print and online, most residents have only a few major financial decisions to make while in training; therefore, they (thankfully) do not yet need to worry about the majority of that content.

This book is designed specifically for medical trainees. We have deliberately limited the content in these pages to cover only the information needed to make the key financial decisions faced during residency. You won't find anything in this book about managing an attending salary or running a practice. This high-yield approach is designed to match the time limitations encountered in residency life. We focus on providing you with the specific information you need to make informed decisions while in training, free from the distractions of less relevant content.

The majority of this book is dedicated to five topics:

1. Education debt
2. Long-term disability insurance
3. Life insurance
4. Investing
5. Financial advisors

A full chapter has been dedicated to each of these topics, as they are each related to a significant financial decision that the majority of residents will encounter during training. In addition to these five topics, we begin with a chapter reviewing "financial vital signs," which can be used to triage your financial situation and set near- and long-term goals. Finally, we conclude with a chapter on financial pearls and pitfalls for residents.

Armed with knowledge and resources to address each of these issues, residents will be empowered to make informed decisions regarding each of the common financial issues that arise during training.

Chapter 1

Financial Vital Signs

Eric Shappell, MD, MHPE

There are four financial vital signs that will help you assess your financial wellbeing in residency:

1. Net worth
2. High-interest debt
3. Credit report and score
4. Emergency fund balance

Checking these vital signs will help you establish a financial baseline and set reasonable short- and long-term financial goals. Tracking these vital signs over time will help you determine how well you are approaching your goals; in addition, this feedback may serve as motivation to maintain or even improve your financial habits. In this section, we will discuss each vital sign and provide examples of relevant goals.

Net Worth

Net worth is simply the value of your assets minus the value of your debts.

$$\text{Net Worth} = \text{Assets} - \text{Debts}$$

Your assets include anything that you own that has a monetary value; for example, checking, savings, and retirement account balances and portions of car and/or property that is paid off would all be considered assets. Debts are any money that you owe, including things you have purchased on payment plans but have not yet paid off. Common examples of resident debts include student loans, credit card debt, and the portions of car(s) and/or property that is not yet paid off.

Most residents will have a significantly negative net worth due to large amounts of education debt. This is not a reason to panic. The purpose of calculating your net worth while in training is to make sure you know your starting point. Tracking your net worth throughout your training will help you ensure that you are meeting your net worth goals.

Depending on how much debt you have, just maintaining your net worth each year can be a formidable goal while in training. While those without significant debt may aim to increase their net worth by a certain amount each year, most residents will not be able to move the needle significantly while in training. Some may even have so much debt that their net worth will almost certainly continue to decrease while in training. However, you can make a tough situation worse by ignoring your net worth and overspending while in residency. Carefully budgeting to minimize spending—particularly on things like housing and cars—and maximize wealth-building (e.g., paying down student loans or, if pursuing Public Service Loan Forgiveness, saving in retirements accounts) can help you optimize your net worth while in training.

High-Interest Debt

High interest debt (>8%) is highly toxic to your net worth. Think of your high-interest debt level like a lactate level. Just like a high lactate almost certainly indicates significant illness, a large amount of high-interest debt almost certainly indicates poor financial health. Clearing your "financial lactate" (i.e., high-interest debt) should be among your top priorities (see page 96 for an example strategy for how to direct your income toward this and other goals).

Credit Report

Credit reports summarize your history of borrowing money, which may include student loans, auto loans, credit cards, or other types of debt. Information on each account's age, type, and payment history can all be found on your credit report.

It is extremely important to check your credit report as you enter residency—when repayment of education loans begins—to make sure that you haven't lost track of any debts. Many students acquire loans from several different loan servicers throughout their educations. Further complicating the matter, education loans can be sold and resold by one loan servicer to another while students are still in school, and many students change addresses during this time period. This large array of factors is a recipe for missed notifications, missed payments, and risk of default. For these reasons, be sure to keep a list of loans and loan servicers so you can send them your new contact information whenever you move, change your phone number, or get a new e-mail address. If you ever lose this list, you can check your federal loan servicers though the National Student Loan Data System website.[5] In addition, all of your creditors—including private loan servicers—will appear on your full credit report, which you can obtain annually for free through AnnualCreditReport.com from each of the three credit bureaus: TransUnion, Experian, and Equifax. Staggering the times that you request a credit report from each bureau will allow you to obtain a free report as frequently as every four months. These reports should be checked regularly—at least annually, and prior to entering residency. Again, this check at the beginning of residency is particularly important, as this is when education loans become due. You do not want to forget about one of your loans and have late payments (or, worse, a default) show up in your credit report and score, since this will negatively impact your ability to obtain credit in the future (e.g., opening a new credit card, refinancing your loans, or securing a mortgage).

Credit Score

Credit scores are a numerical representation of how responsible you are when borrowing money (i.e., paying back money that you owe on time and in full). The score is based on the information in your credit report. In a way, credit scores are like

---

[5] *National Student Loan Data System*. Retrieved from www.nslds.ed.gov/

hemoglobin A1C levels, except instead of measuring your blood sugar levels over the past three months, credit scores measure your borrowing behavior over the past seven years.

There are several factors that go into credit score calculations, including the total amount and types of debt that you have, how long you have had accounts open, how recently you have applied for more credit, and, most importantly, your payment history (on-time payments vs. late payments vs. defaults). There are different scoring models, but the range is typically 300-850, and most residents with education debt can shoot for a credit score of over 700 as a reasonable starting goal.

It is important to measure and track your credit score throughout residency (a reasonable target would be every 4-6 months), as this number is commonly used by lenders and others who are concerned with your financial reliability when you look for a new credit card, apartment, or home. Make sure to use a reputable service to get your credit score—this process typically requires that you input a significant amount of personal information that would make theft of your identity easy if it got in the wrong hands. One reasonable option is to see if you can obtain your credit score through your bank, since some banks are now offering free credit score tracking services to their customers.

Emergency Fund Balance

What is an emergency fund?

An emergency fund is money that you set aside for use only in the case of large, unexpected expenses. Medical or veterinary bills, vehicle repairs, or coverage for monthly household expenses (e.g., rent, utilities, food, insurance) in the case that you need to leave your job or get fired are all expenses that would be covered by an emergency fund. The purpose of an emergency fund is to cover these kinds of critical expenses without needing to take on unfavorable debt (e.g., high-interest credit card debt). There is also value in the peace of mind that many will experience by having this fund in place.

How much should I save in my emergency fund?

The conventional wisdom is to keep 3-6 months of living expenses in your emergency fund. For residents living on approximately $3,000 to $4,000 per month (this range will vary by geography/cost of living and personal lifestyle choices), this comes out to $9,000 to $24,000. The actual amount that you should aim to keep in an emergency fund depends on your specific financial circumstances and risk tolerance, but a reasonable range for most residents is $5,000 to $25,000. Those who have low monthly expenses, multiple streams of income (including, for example, a spouse who also works), and a high risk tolerance may choose to have a relatively small emergency fund. Those who have high monthly expenses (e.g., high cost of living area, childcare), a single revenue stream, and low risk tolerance may choose to aim for a much larger emergency fund. Finally, there are many easily-anticipated life events that are good reasons to temporarily increase your emergency fund. These life events may include moving to a new job and city at the end of residency (which may involve licensing fees, DEA registration, moving expenses, security deposits and broker fees, and a delay in the first check from your new employer), marriage (including the wedding), or expecting a child.

Emergency fund balance as a financial vital sign

When evaluating your emergency fund balance as a financial vital sign, it is important to consider your existing balance as compared with your goal balance (see above). A balance of $12,000 could be too little for some, too much for others, and just right for someone else. It is therefore important to not just check the value of your emergency fund, but to regularly compare it to your current financial circumstances, risk tolerance, and anticipated life events, each of which may vary over time.

Action Items

- ☐ Calculate your net worth (total assets minus total debts).

- ☐ Set a goal for your net worth while in residency based on your budget and level of debt.

- ☐ Calculate the amount of high-interest debt you owe.

- ☐ If you have high-interest debt, make a plan for eliminating it that includes a target date for when it should be gone.

- ☐ Check your credit report and make sure you have set up payments to each of your creditors.

- ☐ Obtain your credit score.

- ☐ Set a goal for your emergency fund balance based on your budget, risk tolerance, and anticipated life events.

- ☐ Calculate the size of your emergency fund compared with your goal.

- ☐ Make a plan (including budget) for how you will reach your emergency fund balance goal that includes a target date for when you should reach it.

Chapter 2

Education Debt

Eric Shappell, MD, MHPE and Michael Ernst, MD

When it comes to federal student loans, there are three main questions that residents need to answer:

Question #1

Should I pursue Public Service Loan Forgiveness (PSLF)?

Question #2

Which loan repayment option should I choose?

Question #3

Should I refinance my loans with a private company?

In this section, we will help you develop a framework for answering these questions based on individual circumstances. Note that in this chapter, we will not discuss other possible but less common loan forgiveness options such as the National Health Service Corps, military service, or employer programs.

> **What is Public Service Loan Forgiveness?**
> Public Service Loan Forgiveness is a program allowing the forgiveness of *qualifying federal loans* after the borrower makes 120 *qualifying payments* while working for a *qualified employer*.

Should I Pursue Public Service Loan Forgiveness?

The first decision to make when developing a loan repayment strategy is whether to pursue Public Service Loan Forgiveness. All remaining steps will be affected by this initial decision. There is no "correct" answer to this question in most cases, but there are some general considerations that can help you decide.

Factors supporting the pursuit of PSLF:
- Qualifying loans
- High debt burden
- Low anticipated 10-year income (including training)
- High likelihood of working at a qualifying employer
- Vigilance
- Risk tolerance

Qualifying Loans

Only Direct federal loans qualify for PSLF.[6] If your loans are from July 1, 2010 or later, your loans should qualify—though you should always check to confirm. If you have federal loans that are not Direct loans (including those before July 1, 2010), you may consolidate them into a Direct loan so that you can begin making qualifying payments on them.

Note that for the purposes of PSLF, consolidated loans will be treated as a new loan. This means that any qualifying payments made to qualifying loans that you then consolidate will not count toward the required 120 PSLF payments, since the count resets to zero for the "new" consolidation loan. For this reason, if you have already made qualifying payments to qualifying loans and you want to keep getting credit for them, it is important to only consolidate your *non-qualifying* loans.

If you haven't made any payments yet, there is still another reason you may want to avoid consolidating all of your loans together, which is related to how the interest rate for the new consolidation loan is calculated. The interest rate for newly consolidated loans will be calculated as the weighted average of the component loans rounded *up* to the nearest 1/8th of a percent. If you have both non-qualifying and qualifying loans and you want to pursue PSLF for all of your loans, you can minimize the effect of this rounding by only consolidating your non-qualifying loans.

---

[6] *Federal Student Aid: Which Types of Federal Student Loans Qualify for PSLF?* Retrieved from https://studentaid.ed.gov/sa/repay-loans/forgiveness-cancellation/public-service#eligible-loans

---

Loan Consolidation Example

Loan A: $100,000 at 5%
Loan B: $100,000 at 6.8%

Weighted average of interest (Loans A and B): 5.9%
Weighted average rounded to nearest 1/8th: 6%

Consolidation loan (Loan A + Loan B): $200,000 at 6%

In summary, you are not required to consolidate all of your loans together. By consolidating only your non-qualifying loans, you can both (1) retain any credit you have earned from qualifying payments to your qualifying loans, and (2) prevent the interest rate on your qualifying loans from being rounded up when averaged with the non-qualifying loans. While there are multiple reasons *not* to consolidate all of your loans together, there is one reason you might want to do this anyway: to enable yourself to begin making qualifying payments earlier in training.

Direct loans have a mandatory six-month grace period during which no qualifying payments can be made. If you consolidate your loans, you can begin making qualifying payments on the consolidation loan right away. Why would you want to start making qualifying payments earlier in training? Your income will likely be lower at the beginning of residency than it will be 10 years later. Since the value you get from PSLF increases as the size of your 120 qualifying payments decreases, making smaller qualifying payments early on will increase your potential benefit from the PSLF program. In addition, your loans will be forgiven six months earlier if you avoid the grace period and begin payments as soon as you enter residency.

High Debt, Low Income

The value of PSLF comes from forgiveness of the remaining balance of your qualifying loans after making 120 qualifying payments. The benefit you receive from this program is greatest for those who have a large amount of debt and can make small qualifying payments, since in this case there will be a lot of unpaid debt left to be forgiven after the 120 qualifying payments. This is why pursuing PSLF may be more appealing for those with a large amount of education debt as compared to those with a small amount.

Since you have to make 120 *qualifying* payments to be eligible for PSLF, you can't just decide to pay a tiny amount each month for 10 years and obtain a large benefit.[7] You have to be enrolled in one of the government's qualifying repayment plans, which will dictate your monthly payment based on the amount of debt you have and your income.

If you make enough money, you will be placed on the standard repayment plan and your required payments will put you on pace to pay off your loans in 10 years. If this is the case from the beginning of your loan repayment, there will be no loans left to forgive at the end of the 10 years (120 payments). Therefore, if you want to benefit from the PSLF program, you need to qualify for and complete income-based payments for at least part of your repayment period—and the longer you're on an income-based plan, the more you will benefit from the program. Luckily, the vast majority of residents and fellows will have income levels low enough to qualify for an income-based repayment plan. Just like with higher debt levels, longer periods

---

[7] *Federal Student Aid: What is a Qualifying Monthly Payment?* Retrieved from https://studentaid.ed.gov/sa/repay-loans/forgiveness-cancellation/public-service#qualifying-payment

of lower pay will increase the amount forgiven after 120 qualifying payments.

Table 2.1 outlines four example cases to compare the amount of loan forgiveness that could be expected in several different debt and income level scenarios. Several assumptions and simplifications were made in these cases; they are meant to be illustrative only and do not represent real scenarios. Case A is designed to represent the type of resident who stands to benefit the most from PSLF: one with a large amount of education debt, a long training period, and a lower attending salary. Case B has the same level of debt but a shorter training period and higher attending income. Cases C and D mirror the training length and attending income levels of Cases A and B, but with a lower starting level of debt.

In summary, those with larger amounts of debt and lower incomes—including longer periods of training—have the greatest potential to benefit from the PSLF program. However, there is typically still some potential benefit to other types of residents. Whether or not the risk of pursuing PSLF is worth the potential benefit, however large or small that may be, is a personal decision.

Table 2.1. Loan forgiveness example cases[8]

	Case A	Case B	Case C	Case D
Starting debt	$300,000	$300,000	$100,000	$100,000
Length of training	6 years	3 years	6 years	3 years
Training income	$50,000	$50,000	$50,000	$50,000
Training payment	$265	$265	$265	$265
Balance after training	$425,000	$355,000	$125,000	$110,000
Attending income	$125,000	$300,000	$125,000	$300,000
Attending payment	$960	$2,825	$960	$2,256
Amount forgiven	**$510,000**	**$270,000**	**$115,000**	**$0**

---

[8] These examples are rough estimates only. They include several assumptions and simplifications in addition to rounding to make comparisons easier. These examples do not represent real scenarios.

Qualified Employers

If considering pursuing PSLF, you should also consider the likelihood that you will work for a qualifying employer[9] for the full 10 years of required PSLF payments. If you don't make 120 payments under a qualifying employer, the program will be of no benefit to you.

Switching to a non-qualifying employer after beginning to pursue PSLF will decrease if not eliminate your potential benefit from the program. This is because you will still be required to make payments on your loans during that time, but those payments won't count towards the forgiveness program, so the amount of qualifying debt that can be forgiven will be reduced. If you don't return to a qualifying employer, or if you do so without enough qualifying loans remaining, you will lose all potential value from the PSLF program.[10] This can come with the additional rub of the missed opportunity to more aggressively pay down debt earlier.

Many hospitals are qualifying organizations; many physician groups are not. Both of these generalities have exceptions. If you are thinking of pursuing PSLF, you should be obtaining this information when applying for jobs after residency.

---

[9] In short, qualifying employers include the government and non-profit 501(c)3 organizations. More information on qualifying employers can be found on the Federal Student Aid website:
https://studentaid.ed.gov/sa/repay-loans/forgiveness-cancellation/public-service

[10] Note that qualifying repayments do not have to be contiguous; you can "leave" and "return to" the program and still have loans forgiven.

Vigilance and Risk Tolerance

Finally, pursuing PSLF requires both vigilance and a degree of risk tolerance. Vigilance is important to maintain certainty that loans, payments, and employers all qualify for the program and are recorded correctly in the loan servicer database. One particularly important pitfall to note is that payments will not qualify for PSLF if you are paid ahead on your loans.[11]

Additionally, the database where payments are recorded is not accessible without contacting the loan servicer to request an audit of your qualifying payments. You should, however, get yearly statements that show the balance of your qualifying payments that are recorded in the database. If you believe there is an error in this automated count, you must request a manual review of your payments. At the time of writing, this process can take close to a full year to complete.

One should not simply trust that the PSLF process is simple and will take care of itself; this is still a relatively new program and is experiencing growing pains. Several horror stories have been reported, including misinterpreted payment plans[12] and invalid approval letters.[13] In fact, since the first wave of borrowers became eligible for forgiveness in the fall of 2017, more than 70% of applications were rejected due to ineligibility and over 25% did not complete the required forms correctly.[14]

---

[11] *Federal Student Aid: Qualifying Payments*. Retrieved from https://studentaid.ed.gov/sa/repay-loans/forgiveness-cancellation/public-service/questions#qualifying-payments

[12] Lieber, R. (2017, 27 October) A Student Loan Nightmare: The Teacher in the Wrong Payment Plan. *The New York Times*, October 27, 2017.

[13] Cowley, S. (2017, 30 March) Student Loan Forgiveness Program Approval Letters May Be Invalid, Education Dept. Says. *The New York Times*.

[14] Berman, J. (2018, 23 September) This government loan forgiveness program has rejected 99% of borrowers so far. *MarketWatch*.

In addition to vigilance regarding repayment status, a degree of risk tolerance is required for two reasons: (1) It is possible that you will want (or need) to switch to a non-qualifying employer before completing 120 payments—thus forfeiting all potential benefit from the program and suffering the missed opportunity to make more aggressive payments early on, and (2) the longevity of the PSLF program itself remains uncertain.[15] The risk that the program may not continue to exist in its current form (or worse, that it could be discontinued) must be taken into account when considering this option.

Which Loan Repayment Option Should I Choose?

There are many options for repayment of federal student loans. Deciding which one to choose can be achieved by answering three questions:

Question #2A
Am I going to pursue PSLF?

Question #2B
How much can I regularly afford to spend on my monthly payments?

Question #2C
Am I disciplined enough to make additional payments?

---

[15] Powell, F. (2017, 3 October) The Fate of Public Service Loan Forgiveness. *U.S. News and World Report.*

Repayment in the Public Service Loan Forgiveness Program

If the answer to the Question #2A is "yes" and you want to maximize the value of the PSLF program, you will need to choose the qualifying income-driven repayment plan that minimizes your loan payments—typically Pay As You Earn (PAYE) or Revised Pay As You Earn (RePAYE).[16] In general, determining the repayment strategy which maximizes the benefit from the PSLF program is simple: Choose the option with the lowest required monthly payment and do not make any additional contributions. Currently, when certifying for income-driven repayment plans, the certification system will offer to automatically select the plan with the lowest monthly payment for you.

RePAYE tends to provide the lowest required monthly payments—10% of discretionary income with a 50% subsidy for unpaid interest—*unless* you're married and your spouse has a high income, in which case using PAYE and filing your taxes separately typically provides the lowest required monthly payment.[17,18] The reason for this is that RePAYE always counts spousal income in calculating your discretionary income, whereas PAYE only counts spousal income if you file taxes jointly. Like RePAYE, PAYE payments are also 10% of discretionary income. However, they do not include an interest subsidy.

---

[16] *Federal Student Aid: What is a Qualifying Repayment Plan?* Retrieved from https://studentaid.ed.gov/sa/repay-loans/forgiveness-cancellation/public-service#qualifying-repayment-plan.

[17] This should *not* be the only factor in deciding how to file your taxes. Consider consulting a tax professional for assistance if you are in this situation.

[18] Lynch et al. *What Should I Do With My Student Loans? A Proposed Strategy for Educational Debt Management.* J Grad Med Educ. 2018 Feb;10(1):11-15.

Note on Deferments

If you will be enrolled in school again during your PSLF repayment period (e.g., a masters or PhD program associated with fellowship) and wish to continue making qualifying payments during this time, be sure to *waive* automatic in-school deferment by completing an In-School Deferment Waiver form, available from your loan servicer. If you do not complete this form prior to enrollment, your loans will automatically be placed in deferment and qualifying payments *will not be made*.

Repayment Without Public Service Loan Forgiveness

Since few residents will be able to afford the Standard Repayment Plan (which is the default option), the choice of repayment plan for residents who are not pursuing PSLF also tends to be limited to income-driven plans. Unlike repayment under PSLF, however, in this scenario, the total loan balance will need to be paid.

When paying off a loan, it is generally in one's long-term interest to make the largest payments possible along the way (thus shortening the life of the loan, which minimizes interest accumulation and the total amount you end up paying). This long-term benefit, however, must be weighed against the short-term cost that comes with larger payments: a tighter budget that limits financial flexibility. Here are three approaches that illustrate each end of this spectrum, including a last-ditch option in case of financial catastrophe:

Approach #1: Maximize regular payments

For those interested in the simplest option, the main consideration is how much can regularly be contributed to loan payments while preserving a sufficient buffer for unexpected expenses (see Question #2B on page 20). As there is no "correct" balance between these two interests, the decision of how much to pay each month will be a personal decision. The more aggressive income-driven repayment option tends to be Income-Contingent Repayment (ICR, typically 20% of discretionary income for residents), while IBR, PAYE, and RePAYE tend to be lower.

Note that most loan servicers will also allow you to schedule supplemental payments on top of your income-driven plan. For example, if you want to contribute $500 per month but your PAYE payment is only $250, you can typically arrange for your loan servicer to deduct an additional $250 from your payment account each month. This is a good option for residents who want to maximize their scheduled payments without the burden of remembering to budget for and make additional contributions themselves.

Approach #2: Maximize flexibility

Another approach is to minimize monthly payments in order to allow maximum financial flexibility. In this case, if a large unexpected expense occurs, you can use the money in your budget that was freed up by smaller monthly loan payments to establish and/or replenish your emergency fund.

In stable times where recovery from unexpected expenses is not necessary, if you are disciplined (see Question #2C on page 20), these funds may be used to make additional payments toward loans. This setup maximizes both flexibility of income and contributions toward loan payments; however, this approach requires a significant amount of attention and discipline—including avoiding spending the additional income on something other than loans and emergency fund recovery. This flexibility may be worth the mental and clerical work to some. Again, the key here is to make sure the money freed up by lower loan payments is being put to good use.

Repayment plans that typically fit this approach include Pay As You Earn (PAYE), Revised Pay As You Earn (RePAYE), or Income-Based Repayment (IBR) plans (depending on the type(s) of loan(s) involved).

Approach #3: Dire financial circumstances

If you are in significant financial trouble, eligible loans can be placed into deferment or forbearance. In both of these situations, payments are halted. Deferment is preferable since the government will continue to pay the interest on your subsidized loans (if you have any); however, specific criteria must be met to qualify for deferment.[19] In forbearance, interest continues to accumulate on all loans. Forbearance also has eligibility criteria, though less restrictive. All residents qualify for forbearance during residency training.

---

[19] For information on deferment and forbearance eligibility criteria, see the federal student aid website: https://studentaid.ed.gov/sa/repay-loans/deferment-forbearance.

Should I Refinance My Loans with a Private Company?

Loan refinancing is the process by which a private company pays off your current loans in exchange for a new loan with new terms that they provide. The primary benefit is that the new interest rate should be lower than the rate charged by the federal government, resulting in less interest over time. If the interest rate offered is not significantly lower than your current interest rate, you probably shouldn't be refinancing.

One of the main factors impacting the interest rate that companies will offer is the monthly payment: As the amount you're willing to commit to paying each month goes up, the interest rate typically goes down (and vice versa). For those with a relatively low income, including most residents and fellows, the amount they are able to commit to paying each month is relatively small; thus, the benefits of refinancing federal student loans tend to be limited. However, exceptions do exist, both in the potential to decrease your interest rate without large monthly payments and in the fact that some residents can afford higher payments. In either of these cases, refinancing loans could save you money.

Whether or not to refinance is a personal decision. However, in general, refinancing is in your best interest if all of the following conditions are met:

Conditions under which to consider refinancing federal loans in residency:

- You do not plan on using the Public Service Loan Forgiveness program *and*
- The interest rate offered is lower than the rate you are currently paying *and*
- You can afford the new monthly payments (which are typically higher) *and*
- You do not expect any foreseeable economic hardships over the course of your repayment period (refinanced loans are private loans and thus cannot be placed back into deferment, forbearance, or any other government repayment plan).

Refinancing with Variable vs. Fixed Interest Rates

Most companies offer both fixed and variable interest rate loans. Interest rates on fixed loans do not change over the lifetime of the loan. Variable interest rate loans tend to be offered at lower initial rates than fixed loans; however, the interest rate on a variable loan can increase or decrease over time (usually these rates are tied to an index, such as the one-month London Interbank Offered Rate or LIBOR).

There is no way to know which type of interest rate will turn out to be the cheapest. However, in general, the shorter the repayment period, the less risk a variable loan presents. For example, let's say you had $100,000 in loans at a variable rate of 4% that jumps to and remains at 8%. The increased cost from the higher interest rate if that loan is paid off over five years is $11,160 ($110,520 at 4% vs. $121,680 at 8%), whereas the increased cost if the loan is paid off over 10 years is $24,120

($121,440 at 4% vs. $145,560 at 8%) and over 20 years is $55,200 ($145,440 at 4% vs $200,640 at 8%).

Since most residents don't have room in their budget for payments large enough to pay off a loan in five years, they would need longer loan periods that are more vulnerable to increases in variable interest rates. For this reason, refinancing into a variable rate loan as a resident—particularly early in residency—will usually come with significant risk.

In summary, deciding whether to choose a fixed or variable interest rate repayment plan is personal and should be based on individual risk tolerance and the length of the expected repayment period. Factors that favor a fixed interest rate include a longer repayment period (10-plus years) and a desire to minimize risk.

Note on Refinancing

When pricing out loan refinancing options, most companies will require you to enter personal information and will run a credit check to help determine which rates to offer you, if any.

Most of these credit checks will be what is called a "soft inquiry" or "soft pull," which means they will request some of the information from your credit report. These "soft pulls" will *not* affect your credit score.

Some lenders, however, will perform a "hard inquiry" or "hard pull" during the pricing process. "Hard pulls" will lower your credit score and typically stay on your credit report for a few years. Therefore, when pricing out refinancing options, make sure that the company is only performing a "soft pull" in the pricing process unless you are ready to sign with the company and this is a required part of the process.

Summary

Should I pursue Public Service Loan Forgiveness?

If you have a large amount of qualifying loans, a high likelihood of working at a qualifying employer (i.e., government or non-profit organization), and especially if you have a long training period (5-plus years), you should consider PSLF. However, the future of the program is uncertain.

Which loan repayment option should I choose?

If you're pursuing PSLF, pay as little as you can—the less you pay, the greater the benefit of PSLF. Think RePAYE unless your spouse has a high income, in which case you may consider PAYE while filing taxes separately.[20] If you're not pursuing PSLF, choose a plan where you're paying as much as you can afford.

Should I refinance my loans with a private company?

Definitely not if you're pursuing PSLF, but still probably not while you're in residency. To get the main benefit of refinancing (i.e., a lower interest rate), companies usually want shorter repayment periods with higher monthly payments. Most residents can't afford that. Plus, federal loans have perks like deferment and forbearance if you run into financial problems. If you are absolutely sure that you will not be pursuing PSLF and you can secure a significantly lower interest rate with payments you can afford, refinancing is a reasonable option.

---

[20] Again, this should *not* be the only factor in deciding how to file your taxes. Consider consulting a tax professional for assistance if considering this option.

Action Items

- ☐ Determine which federal loans you owe using the National Student Loan Data System[21] (Note: This will not include any private loans you may have).

- ☐ Pick (or confirm) your repayment plan.

- ☐ If you are pursuing or might pursue PSLF, complete the employer certification form[22] once every year.

- ☐ If you are certain that you are *not* pursuing PSLF, consider refinancing your loans.

---

[21] *Federal Student Aid.* Retrieved from https://www.nslds.ed.gov/
[22] *Public Service Loan Forgiveness (PSLF): Employment Certification Form.* (2018) Retrieved from
https://studentaid.ed.gov/sa/sites/default/files/public-service-employment-certification-form.pdf

Chapter 3

Long-Term Disability Insurance

Michael Ernst, MD and Eric Shappell, MD, MHPE

The purpose of long-term disability (LTD) insurance is to financially support you and your dependents in the event that you are unable to work as you currently do. Disabilities that can affect your ability to work range from chronic medical conditions (e.g., cancer or low back pain), to accidents (e.g., a hand injury from rock climbing), to mental health issues (e.g., depression or alcoholism).

While short-term disabilities are commonly covered by cash reserves (though short-term disability insurance is also available for purchase), long-term disabilities have significant potential to affect one's finances. Thus, insurance to protect against this possibility warrants special consideration.

Five questions can help residents navigate decisions related to LTD insurance, each of which will be addressed in this chapter:

Question #1

Should I buy long-term disability insurance in residency?

Question #2

What are the different types of long-term disability insurance?

Question #3

Which properties of long-term disability insurance should I consider?

Question #4

Where can I buy long-term disability insurance?

Question #5

How much will my long-term disability insurance policy cost?

Should I Buy Long-Term Disability Insurance in Residency?

This question boils down to two factors: budget and risk tolerance. Physical or mental disabilities have the potential to be financially devastating, particularly early in one's career. Estimates of the probability of becoming disabled are widely varied, but approximately 15% of working adults will have a period of disability before age 65 and the average length of an LTD claim before recovery is approximately three years. For this reason, at least some form of LTD insurance is highly recommended for those who can afford it.

Budget

Residents have highly variable financial circumstances, so this coverage may fit into some budgets but not others. For residents who are well-off financially, it might make sense to purchase a strong—but, accordingly, expensive—individual policy. Other residents may decide that they can only afford a less-robust individual policy or their group policy while in training. Residents who are struggling financially (e.g., those with a significant amount of high-interest debt) may choose to defer the purchase of LTD insurance until their circumstances improve.

Risk Tolerance

The prior section assumes that residents want to fit LTD insurance into their budget; however, this isn't always the case. While some residents may highly value the sense of security that comes with a high-end, air-tight LTD insurance policy and be willing to cut other costs to make room in their budgets for it, others who could easily afford it may still not find this type of policy to be worth the expense. It only makes sense to buy the amount of coverage that you feel you need to be comfortable given your overall financial plan, budget, and capacity for risk.

In addition to the risk of becoming disabled, there is also a risk of losing the ability to be covered for certain conditions due to events that have occurred before you purchase insurance. For example, if during residency you see a psychiatrist about an episode of depression or a primary care doctor about low back pain after a car accident, you may find insurance companies unwilling to cover you for mental health or musculoskeletal complaints in the future. If you entered residency in good health and purchased a policy before these events, however, these conditions would likely still be covered under that policy. In short, the longer you wait to purchase a policy, the greater the risk that something will happen to you that will limit your future insurability.

What Are the Different Types of Long-Term Disability Insurance?

There are two types of long-term disability insurance that are generally applicable to residents: individual policies and group policies. Disability coverage is also offered through the federal government, but the government definition is so strict and the benefits so relatively small that residents who are interested in meaningful disability insurance should look further.

Individual vs. Group Policies

Terms of individual policies are customizable to meet your specific needs; this usually makes individual policies more desirable than group policies in all areas except one—cost. Individual policies tend to be significantly more expensive than group policies.

There are three main areas in which individual policies might make this expense worthwhile:

1. Strength of the definition of disability[23]
2. Total available coverage (e.g., benefit amount, benefit length)
3. Portability (i.e., the policy continues to cover you even if you switch jobs)[24]

These three areas have been highlighted because group disability insurance policies rarely include all three (i.e., a strong definition of disability, a high benefit amount that will pay out over many years, and portability in the case that you leave that group). However, it is important to read the terms of your group policy carefully since some employers may offer exceptionally strong group options that may turn out to be favorable alternatives to individual policies (particularly when accounting for cost).

---

[23] Individual policies do not have intrinsically strong definitions of disability (i.e., they are not guaranteed to be inclusive in what is considered "disabled"); it is up to the purchaser to choose a policy with a suitable definition for their needs.

[24] Portability and guaranteed continuation of the policy requires that the policy is non-cancellable, guaranteed renewable, and that premiums are paid on time.

What Properties of Long-Term Disability Insurance Should I Consider?

There are all kinds of different properties that can be included in LTD insurance policies. While an exhaustive discussion of these features is beyond the scope of this book, we will highlight a few key properties that residents should consider, stratified by priority.

High Priority Policy Features

Own-Occupation, Specialty-Specific

This is arguably the most important part of the LTD insurance policy.

With an "any occupation" definition of disability, you are only considered disabled if you can't perform the duties of *any* occupation for which you are qualified. For example, you would not receive benefits if you can work as a bank teller instead of a physician. This is how disability is defined for social security benefits.

An "own-occupation" definition provides a stronger definition of disability, allowing you to receive benefits even if you are still able to function in a different occupation.

A definition that is "specialty-specific" is even stronger, allowing you to receive benefits even if you are still able to function as a physician in a different specialty (e.g., as an urgent care doctor instead of a medical intensivist).

If it is important to you that benefits are paid if you are unable to practice in your current job, pay close attention to the language in this area and look for these terms.

Which specialty is covered if I later sub-specialize?

The "specialty-specific" policy language typically reads that you will be covered if you can't perform the duties of the medical specialty you were practicing just prior to becoming disabled. This means that if you buy a specialty-specific policy as an internal medicine resident but become disabled later as an interventional cardiologist, you would receive benefits if you could not perform the duties of an interventional cardiologist—even if you could still practice internal medicine. Be sure to review and discuss this policy language with your agent to be sure you're purchasing the policy you want.

Non-Cancellable and Guaranteed Renewable

These terms mean that the insurance company can't change the price, benefit, or other terms of your policy so long as you pay the premiums.

Nice-to-Have Policy Features

Future Purchase Option

You won't be able to purchase enough insurance to cover your attending-level income as a resident—most companies will cap you at a benefit of $5,000-6,000 per month while in residency, which is usually much less than the typical cap for attendings (60% of their salary). A future purchase option rider will allow you to buy additional coverage once your income increases without a medical screening exam or lifestyle questionnaire. This can allow you to cover an appropriate amount of attending-level income under the terms of your current policy, even if something happens before exercising the future purchase option that might otherwise affect your insurability (e.g., treatment for depression or low back pain, as discussed on page 34).

Note that this is a future *purchase* option—not a free increase in benefit when your income goes up; the amount that you increase your benefit will be accompanied by an increase in your premium. Note also that this is a future purchase *option*—not a requirement; if you decide as an attending to get additional coverage through your employer rather than exercising this option on your individual policy, your premiums will not increase.

Cost of Living Adjustment

Due to inflation, the buying power of the $5,000-per-month benefit that you purchase when you're 30 will be significantly less by the time you're 60 (in fact, the buying power will be just under $2,400 assuming the rate of inflation is 2.5%). Particularly when you're young and there are many years for inflation to eat away at the value of your benefit, you may want to consider a Cost of Living Adjustment Rider. This rider is designed to protect the purchasing power of your benefit by increasing it by a predetermined percentage each year; typically, this percentage is linked to the Consumer Price Index (CPI) and maxes out somewhere around 3-6%.

Note that cost of living adjustments only take effect if the policy owner becomes disabled and starts collecting the benefit. If you purchase this rider and remain healthy, the benefit amount will not increase.[25]

---

[25] There is a type of policy feature that will increase your benefit amount each year for the first few years you own the policy—even if you are not collecting benefits. This feature is typically called an "automatic increase benefit," or something similar. These benefit increases come with an increase in the premium that you have to pay.

Additional Notes

Within your policy, you will be able to set the waiting period before your benefits kick in (typically 90 days) and the age through which your benefits will pay out (typically age 65). You can adjust each of these properties, which will result in changes to your premium (e.g., shorter waiting periods are more expensive, as are higher ages through which benefits would be paid).

Examples

Here are three examples of how residents may approach LTD insurance while in in training:

Example A

Given the expense of high-end individual policies, Alex chooses to purchase a basic individual policy during residency with a plan to purchase more comprehensive individual coverage at the end of residency, when close to making an attending salary.

Example B

Financially well-off with a high-income spouse but still wanting income protection, Jesse decides to purchase a high-end individual policy during residency, including a Cost of Living Adjustment rider and future purchase option to increase the amount of coverage under this policy at a later date, when making an attending salary.

Example C

More concerned about day-to-day expenses than the possibility of becoming disabled during residency, Pat chooses to purchase LTD insurance through the hospital's group policy since this was the most affordable option available. Pat plans to purchase an individual policy just prior to graduation from residency.

Where Can I Buy Long-Term Disability Insurance?

Group Policies

Most residents' employers will offer group long-term disability insurance policies. Details of this process should be available through the Benefits Office or Human Resources department. Group policies may have limitations on enrollment periods (e.g., coverage must be purchased within 30 days of beginning employment or during annual enrollment periods). If coverage is available for purchase outside of standard enrollment periods, there may be additional requirements (e.g., these applications may be subject to medical screening exams whereas new employee applications may not). Check the terms of your group's policy if you are considering this option.

Individual Policies

Individual LTD policies must be purchased through agents. If you purchase a policy through an agent, make sure that he or she is willing and able to sell you policies from any company (i.e., ensure the agent is not beholden to a certain company that may not have the best policy for you). Most training programs have at least one financially-inclined faculty member who should be able to recommend a local agent. Alternatively, websites like The White Coat Investor host lists of insurance agents from which you can choose. [26]

---

[26] *The White Coat Investor: Insurance Agents for Physicians.* (2018) Retrieved from https://www.whitecoatinvestor.com/websites-2/insurance/

You may find yourself feeling pressured to purchase additional products or add-ons when you meet with a financial advisor or insurance salesperson. You can minimize these pressures by coming prepared (having a written plan helps), firmly stating exactly what you would like to purchase, and sticking to your guns when other offers start coming up. If you feel that the agent has made a good point and you are considering purchasing more than you came for, there is no harm in writing down the information and taking it home with you to think about before making a purchase. If you have time, it may also be worthwhile to shop around with different agents to ensure you are getting the best deal possible.

Finally, if you ever feel uncomfortable with an agent, walk out and find a new one. There are plenty of agents out there who would be happy to sell you a long-term disability insurance policy.

How Much Will My Long-Term Disability Insurance Policy Cost?

Group Policies

Premiums for group policies are typically calculated using multipliers (i.e., the total income that will be covered is multiplied by a constant agreed upon by the group). The range of multipliers may be very wide depending on the strength of the policy. Multipliers may be over 1% for strong policies and closer to 0.1% for weaker policies. For a benefit that pays 60% of a $60,000 resident salary, this comes out to a premium of around $5 to $50 per month ($60 to $600 per year) for a benefit of $3,000 per month ($36,000 per year). These estimates are also featured in Table 3.1.

Group LTD insurance premiums are typically paid with pre-tax income. Therefore, the benefits paid in the event you become disabled would be subject to taxation.

Individual Policies

Individual policies will also range widely in price depending on the terms of the policy (e.g., definition of disability, length of eligibility, future purchase options and Cost of Living Adjustment riders, etc.). Most policies for residents that include strong terms will run from 2 to 5% of the benefit amount. Since most residents will only qualify for a benefit of approximately $5,000 per month, this comes out to a premium of around $100 to $250 per month ($1,200 to $3,000 per year). See Table 3.1 for comparisons of estimated group and individual LTD policy rates. Individual disability insurance policies are typically paid with post-tax income, therefore the benefits paid in the event you become disabled are not taxed.

Table 3.1. Comparison of example group and individual rates

Type	Price	Monthly Benefit	Monthly Premium	Cost Index
Group	Inexpensive	$3,000	$5	0.17%
	Expensive	$3,000	$50	1.67%
Individual	Inexpensive	$5,000	$100	2.00%
	Expensive	$5,000	$250	5.00%

Note: These rough estimates are for illustration only and do not represent any real policies. The group benefit assumes 60% coverage for a $60,000 salary ($3,000); the individual benefit assumes purchase of the maximum amount typically available to residents ($5,000). Cost index is the premium divided by the benefit. Whereas premiums for group policies tend to be paid with pre-tax earnings and therefore benefits are subject to income tax, individual policies are normally paid with post-tax dollars and have tax-free benefits.

Summary

Should I buy long-term disability insurance in residency?

Probably. Around 15% of working adults will have a period of disability before age 65, and the average length of a claim before recovery is approximately three years, which is long enough to be financially devastating for most. At least some coverage to protect against this possibility seems prudent. You don't need to break the bank over a fancy policy; just like you probably live in the apartment you can *afford* rather than the one you *want* during residency, so too can your LTD insurance policy be matched to your budget during training. With that said, you do not need disability insurance if you think you would be ok without your income if you became disabled (e.g., if you have a high-income spouse that would keep working).

What are the different types of long-term disability insurance?

Group and individual. Group policies are typically offered through your employer, whereas individual policies are purchased on your own. Individual policies typically have more to offer but are also typically more expensive.

What properties of long-term disability insurance I should consider?

Look for a policy that is non-cancellable, guaranteed renewable, and, unless you'd be fine with doing some other job, own-occupation that is specialty-specific. Cost of Living Adjustment riders and future purchase options are also nice, particularly early in your career. These options may not be available from group policies, but should be available through an individual policy.

Where can I buy long-term disability insurance?

Find an agent who can sell you policies from multiple companies. Your colleagues in your program can likely recommend someone with whom they have had a positive experience. You can also easily find agents online.

How much will my long-term disability insurance policy cost?

As a rough estimate, the premium may be 0.2-2.0% of the benefit covered for group policies and 2.0-5.0% of the benefit covered for individual policies.

Action Items

☐ Determine what kind of long-term disability insurance is offered by your employer (this may involve calling your Benefits Office or Human Resources).

☐ Decide which kind of long-term disability insurance you would like to purchase (if any) and when you would like purchase it.

☐ Find an insurance agent who can sell you policies from multiple companies and price out various options to compare companies and features.

☐ Purchase your LTD insurance policy.

Chapter 4

Life Insurance

Michael Ernst, MD and Eric Shappell, MD, MHPE

The purpose of life insurance is to financially support your dependents in the event of your death. Five questions can help residents navigate decisions about life insurance, each of which will be addressed in this chapter:

Question #1
Should I buy life insurance during residency?

Question #2
What type of life insurance should I buy?

Question #3
How much life insurance should I buy?

Question #4
Where can I buy life insurance?

Question #5
How much will my life insurance policy cost?

Should I Buy Life Insurance During Residency?

In most cases, this question is interchangeable with the question: "Does anyone depend on me financially?" This is most commonly a spouse and/or children, but could also include parents or others. If the answer to this question is yes, purchasing life insurance can help you financially support these dependents in the unlikely event of your death.

Residents may also be interested in purchasing life insurance if they expect to have financial dependents in the future and want to lock in a rate and coverage while they are still young and healthy.

If your only concern is the balance of your federal student loans, you do not need life insurance. These loans are discharged upon proof of death. Note that this is not always the case with loans held by private companies (e.g., loans that have been refinanced). If you have private loans, check with your loan servicer to determine if these loans are dischargeable upon death. If they aren't, you should factor these loans into your calculations of how much life insurance to buy (see page 51 for more on calculating life insurance needs).

What Type of Life Insurance Should I Buy?

For residents who answered "yes" to Question #1, the answer for nearly everyone is simple: level term. Most other types of policies mix investment with insurance and offer a lower value than you would get from handling each of these separately. In this section, we will briefly outline life insurance policy terminology (see Table 4.1), types of policies, and key features of each policy type. This information has been included to provide an overview of the life insurance landscape; however, unless you have highly unique financial circumstances, know that a term policy is likely to be most affordable and offer the best value for financially protecting your dependents in the unlikely event of your death.

Table 4.1. Life insurance terminology

Term	Description
Premium	The payment required from the insured at a defined interval (e.g., monthly, quarterly, or yearly) throughout the duration of the policy
Death Benefit	The amount of money paid to the beneficiary upon the death of the insured
Cash Value	Money accumulated through permanent life insurance that is independent of the death benefit

Types of Life Insurance Policies

There are two main categories of life insurance: term and permanent.

Term

The defining characteristic of term policies is that they offer a predetermined death benefit for a specific period of time (i.e., the policy term), after which they expire. There is no cash value in term policies.

Permanent

Permanent policies do not automatically expire and can be maintained throughout the entire life of the insured, provided that premiums are paid. Permanent policies also have a cash value component. These policies are a mixture of investment and insurance products, the price of which is typically higher than dealing with each of these financial areas separately. Accordingly, permanent life insurance is not recommended for residents. Table 4.2 compares several characteristics of different life insurance policy types.

Summary

The realm of life insurance can get quite complicated. Again, though—unless you have highly unique financial circumstances as a resident, level term insurance is likely most appropriate option for financially protecting your dependents in the event of your death.

Table 4.2. Types of life insurance policies

Type	Subtype	Characteristics		
		Premiums	Death Benefit	Cash Value
Term	Decreasing	Fixed	Decreasing	None
	Level	Fixed	Fixed	None
	Increasing	Increasing	Increasing	None
Permanent	Whole	Fixed	Fixed	Increasing
	Universal	Variable	Fixed/Variable	Variable
	Variable	Variable	Variable	Variable

How Much Life Insurance Should I Buy?

The purpose of life insurance is to financially protect your dependents in the event of your death; accordingly, your dependents' anticipated financial needs should be used as a benchmark when calculating how much life insurance you should buy. Most physician life insurance policies will be measured in millions.

Calculating Life Insurance Needs

The crudest commonly-used estimate for life insurance coverage needs is 10 times your annual salary. This type of estimate fails to account for a number of personal factors and could over- or underestimate your insurance needs.

A more specific estimate can be made by adding up existing debts, monthly expenses, and anticipated one-time expenses such as college tuition or funeral costs, then subtracting your assets that can be applied to these costs and any income that will remain after your death (e.g., spousal income).

There are many life insurance need calculators available for free online (e.g., the Life Happens Insurance Need Calculator[27]). These calculators can be helpful when estimating your own life insurance needs. Finally, as with all insurance decisions, each of these estimates may need to be adjusted for personal risk tolerance.

---

[27] Life Happens. (2017) Retrieved from
http://www.lifehappens.org/insurance-overview/life-insurance/calculate-your-needs/

Policy Layering

One of the nice things about life insurance policies is that you aren't limited to just one policy. A common reason that you might want more than one policy is that you anticipate the amount of coverage you will need will decrease over time. This scenario assumes that you will be building up your wealth as you work over the years. As your personal wealth builds, your need for insurance declines, since the personal wealth you've accumulated can be used to provide for your family. In addition, the amount of time for which you will need your death benefit to cover dependents' expenses (i.e., the time to their financial independence, retirement, or death) will be decreasing over that same interval. To account for these changes in needs, one option is to buy multiple life insurance policies with different term lengths. See Example A in Figure 4.1 for a graphical depiction of this concept. Before buying two different life insurance policies with different terms, however, be sure to compare the price of their combined premiums to the price of a single large policy with the longer term. For example, in the case shown in Example A of Figure 4.1, the combined premiums of Policy 1 and Policy 2 should be compared to the premium of $2 million 30-year term policy. If the prices are similar, you may end up choosing to go with the extra coverage provided by the larger single policy. Only consider splitting policies that you can otherwise afford if it is going to save you money.

A modification of this approach can also be used to make life insurance more affordable during residency. For example, if a general surgery resident calculates that he or she would need $2 million in insurance to cover future expenses for his or her spouse and children but the premiums for that policy would be very difficult to afford, he or she could purchase a cheaper $1 million policy to ensure some immediate coverage with plans to purchase an additional $1 million in coverage upon graduation from residency.[28]

Taking this example further, if the general surgery resident believes that they will have built up enough wealth after 20 years working as an attending that they estimate the needs of their spouse and children at that time would be only $1 million, they could save money on the second policy by selecting a shorter term (i.e., 20 years as opposed to 30 years). This is depicted graphically in Example B in Figure 4.1.

While ideally all financial needs would be insured at all times, this approach can enable residents with tighter budgets who might not otherwise be able to afford life insurance to get on the board with some coverage while awaiting their attending salaries.

---

[28] Note that purchase of this second policy at a later date will require that the resident go through the process of medical underwriting again.

Figure 4.1. Policy Layering

Policy	Term	Death Benefit
Policy 1	30 years	$1 million
Policy 2	20 years	$1 million

Example A

Age	30-34	35-39	40-44	45-49	50-54	55-59	60-64
Policy Years	1-5	6-10	11-15	16-20	21-25	26-30	31-35
Policy 1							
Policy 2							
Total Death Benefit	$2M	$2M	$2M	$2M	$1M	$1M	$0

Example B

Age	30-34	35-39	40-44	45-49	50-54	55-59	60-64
Policy Years	1-5	6-10	11-15	16-20	21-25	26-30	31-35
Policy 1							
Policy 2							
Total Death Benefit	$1M	$2M	$2M	$2M	$2M	$1M	$0

Where Can I Buy Life Insurance?

Once you've calculated the death benefit and term length that you need, it's time to buy the policy. Most policies will be purchased through agents. Like with purchasing LTD insurance, if you plan to purchase a life insurance policy through an agent, make sure that he or she is willing and able to sell you policies from any company (i.e., ensure the agent is not beholden to a certain company that may not have the best policy for you). Again, most training programs have at least one financially-inclined faculty member who should be able to recommend a local agent. Alternatively, websites like term4sale.com will give the contact information of local agents, in addition to policy pricing, for free. Don't be afraid to shop around and get multiple quotes from different agents.

Think of purchasing term life insurance from an agent like ordering an entrée from an enthusiastic waiter: Even if you give the waiter your exact order, he or she may try to up-sell you an appetizer, something to drink, and a dessert. Similarly, when you approach an insurance agent requesting a 30-year level-term policy with a $500,000 death benefit, the agent may to try to sell you some disability insurance, whole life insurance, and an annuity while you're there. Again, you can minimize these pressures by coming prepared (having a written plan helps), firmly stating exactly what you would like to purchase, and sticking to your guns when the other offers start coming up. If you feel that the agent has made a good point and you are considering purchasing more than you came for, there is no harm in writing down the information and taking it home with you to think about before making a purchase.

As always, if you ever feel uncomfortable with an agent, walk out and find a new one. There are plenty of agents out there who would be happy to sell you a life insurance policy.

How Much Will My Life Insurance Policy Cost?

The cost of your life insurance policy will depend on the amount you want covered, the term length, and your risk (i.e., age, health, smoking status, etc.).

At the time of writing (Summer 2018), there are several reasonable options for a 30-year-old non-smoking female to buy a $1M 30-year policy for $520-550 per year. A similar policy for a male resident is around $675 per year.

You can get free estimates of what your policy will cost online without the need to input your contact information (e.g., term4sale.com). If the insurance agent quotes you a number that is significantly different from the estimate you see, be sure to clarify that the policy does not contain any additional riders that may increase the price (e.g., that premiums will be waived in the case of disability). The quotes you receive will be contingent upon your passing a medical screening exam, which typically involves a representative scheduling an appointment at your home to take blood and urine samples and filling out a medical history and lifestyle questionnaire.

Summary

Should I buy life insurance?

If you have people who depend on your income, yes. If you plan to have people who depend on your income and you want to lock in rates and coverage while young and healthy, yes. Otherwise, no—at least not yet.

What kind of life insurance should I buy?

For most, level term insurance with a term of 20 or 30 years is reasonable.

How much life insurance should I buy?

This should be calculated (see page 51 for a discussion of how to do this), but most residents will likely be buying policies in the $1-3 million range.

Where can I buy life insurance?

A local agent recommended by a colleague, review service (e.g., Yelp), or online database (e.g., Term4Sale.com).

How much will my life insurance policy cost?

At the time of writing (Summer 2018), there are several reasonable options for a 30-year-old non-smoking female to buy a $1M 30-year policy for $520-550 per year. A similar policy for a male resident is around $675 per year.

Action Items

☐ Decide whether to buy life insurance during residency based on current and/or anticipated financial dependents.

☐ Estimate the amount of level term life insurance you need to buy.

☐ Price out policies from different companies online.

☐ Contact a local agent to sell you a policy at the price point you find online.

Chapter 5

Investing

Matthew Pirotte, MD and Eric Shappell, MD, MHPE

Investing is a key component of growing your net worth. In short, investing is the practice of spending money with the expectation that your purchase will grow in value. The most common form of investing is through stock and bond markets; however, many other types of investments exist. We will discuss investing for residents in three parts:

Part 1
Should I be investing during residency?

Part 2
The language of investing

Part 3
Practical applications

Should I Be Investing During Residency?

Budgeting

The first step in answering this question is to create a detailed budget that accounts for all income and expenses. It is important to budget at least a small amount of money "left over" after expenses each month to allow replenishing of your emergency fund after an unforeseen expense—maintaining a full emergency fund is a top priority. In times where your emergency fund is full and you do not have unforeseen expenses, this surplus of income can be used for other purposes, such as investing or making supplemental student loan payments.

Choice

If you have money left over after paying expenses and your emergency fund is at goal, the next step is deciding whether this leftover income should be invested, used to pay down education debt, or used for another purpose. We will assume that residents want to use these funds for wealth building and therefore will focus on the decision between investing and making additional payments toward student loans. This line of reasoning also assumes that there is no high-interest debt (>8%) to which funds should likely be applied before considering investing or making additional loan payments.

The decision whether to invest or pay down student loans is complex and does not have one "correct" answer, but there are a few guiding principles:

Situations favoring investing:

- Pursuing Public Service Loan Forgiveness

  The benefit of the Public Service Loan Forgiveness (PSLF) program is greatest when you pay as little as possible toward your loans in the 10-year payment period.

- Employer Match

  If your employer has a match (i.e., if your employer will contribute extra money to your retirement account when you contribute a portion of your paycheck), the appeal of investing at least enough to get the full match is significantly increased.

- Low-Interest Loans

  The lower your student loan interest rate, the more likely it is that investing will turn out to be the best decision for growing your net worth. This is by no means guaranteed; there is always the risk of low returns (or even losses) when investing.

- No Loans

  Residents without student loans or other significant debt should strongly consider investing.

Situations favoring supplemental loan payments:

- High-Interest Loans

  If your student loans have a high interest rate (i.e., more than ~8%), it is likely that making additional student loan payments will turn out to be the best decision for growing your net worth. This is assuming you are not pursuing PSLF.

- Desire for Guaranteed "Returns"

  When making properly-applied supplemental loan payments,[29] you are guaranteed that the principal (i.e., the amount of money that is collecting interest) will go down. This guarantees a "return" of your payment amount at the loan's interest rate (e.g., $500 at 6.8%). There is no telling what would happen to that same amount of money if you invest it in the stock market—it could perform the same, better, or much worse. There is value in a guaranteed return on investment.

Each of the above factors needs to be considered in the context of personal risk tolerance and overall financial profile in order to decide whether to invest during residency. While many residents will decide they can't afford to invest or choose to use their extra money for other purposes (e.g., paying down education debt), some will choose to start investing. The remainder of this chapter will discuss the basics of investing with a focus on types of investments and investment accounts that are suitable for residents.

---

[29] Properly-applied supplemental loan payments are those that pay down the loan principal; they are not applied to loan interest.

The Language of Investing

Just like the world of medicine, the world of finance has its own language. All the different terms and acronyms can be intimidating, thus discouraging residents from learning more. While it is true that one could spend weeks learning the language of investing in detail, fortunately, the financial situations of most residents are simple enough that only a few key concepts need to be understood in order to make sound investment decisions.

One of the early hang-ups for residents is understanding the relationship between types of investment *accounts* and types of *investments*. An analogy that can be helpful in understanding this relationship is that of a grocery store: In this analogy, investment accounts can be thought of as the grocery bags, and individual investments are the groceries. This is graphically represented in Figure 5.1.

Just like you can pick whichever loaf of bread you want and put it in whichever available bag you want, so too can you buy any stock and put it in any available account. There are some income and employment restrictions on which accounts (bags) are available at any given time, but most residents will have several good options.

Figure 5.1. Grocery store analogy for types of accounts and investments

Accounts	Investments
Roth IRA	Stock X
401(k)	Bond Y
Taxable	Mutual Fund Z

Types of Accounts

There are four types of investment accounts that residents are likely to consider: 401(k), 403(b), Roth IRA, and Traditional IRA. For reference, we will also briefly comment on taxable (brokerage) accounts. The most significant difference between investment accounts is how they are taxed.

Important questions to ask when considering the tax treatment of accounts include:

- *Are my contributions to the account going to be taxed as they go in?*

- *Do my investments in the account grow tax-free?*

- *Is the money I withdraw from the account taxed on the way out?*

- *Are there penalties if I withdraw the money before a certain amount of time?*

All of the investment accounts that are most suitable for residents—401(k), 403(b), and Roth IRA—are retirement accounts.[30] Each of these accounts has the benefit of tax-free growth of investments, whereas growth in "taxable," also known as "brokerage" accounts (which are not retirement accounts), is taxed.

A 401(k) or 403(b) is a retirement account that is provided by an employer. IRAs, or Individual Retirement Accounts, are retirement accounts that are created and managed by you as an individual. For residents opening an IRA (including a Roth IRA), know that contributions are limited for incomes that exceed a certain amount, depending on whether you file taxes as an individual or jointly with a spouse.[31]

Retirement accounts do differ in how investments are taxed "going in" (contributions) and "coming out" (withdrawals).

---

[30] Traditional IRAs are also retirement accounts, but they are less suitable for residents because they will cause problems with utilizing backdoor Roth IRAs in the future.

[31] For up-to-date information on IRA contribution and income limits, visit the IRS website: https://www.irs.gov/retirement-plans.

Table 5.1 outlines the different tax treatments of several retirement accounts as well as taxable accounts.

In general, if you hear the term "Roth" referring to a 401(k), 403(b), or IRA, it means contributions are taxed but earnings and qualified withdrawals are tax-free. A Roth account can be advantageous for those who expect their income to go up in the future (e.g., residents), because taxes can be paid now, while in a lower tax bracket, as opposed to in the future, when they are expected to be in a higher tax bracket.

Matching

Also outlined in Table 5.1 is whether different accounts are eligible for a "match." In short, a *match* is an amount of money that your employer pays into your retirement account for you—with a catch: You need to contribute a certain amount yourself to get it. For example, if your employer offers a 3% match and you put 3% of your paycheck into your 403(b), they will match your contribution and you will end up with a total of 6% of your paycheck's value added to your 403(b) account. If you only put in 1.5% of your paycheck, your employer will match your contribution and you will end up with 3% of your paycheck's value added to your account.

Matching is a feature of many (but not all) retirement plans that are offered by employers (e.g., 401(k) and 403(b) accounts). Roth IRAs, Traditional IRAs, and taxable accounts are all individual accounts that you set up and manage yourself. There is no employer match for individual accounts.

A match is a great benefit; unfortunately, not many organizations offer a match for their medical trainees. However, if your employer does offer this benefit, you should strongly consider contributing enough of your salary to get the full match from your employer.

Table 5.1. Types of Accounts (Grocery bags)

Account Type	Possible Match	Contributions Taxed	Withdrawal Taxed	Suitable for Residents
Traditional 401(k) / 403(b)	Yes	No	Yes	Maybe
Roth 401(k) / 403(b)	Yes	Yes	No	Usually
Roth IRA	No	Yes	No	Usually
Traditional IRA	No	No	Yes	No
Taxable	No	Yes	Yes	No

Vesting

Note that, in addition to requiring you contribute a certain amount to get the match, some employers also have a *vesting period*.

In short, a vesting period is an amount of time that you need to work for a company before the company's contribution (i.e., the match) belongs to you. While leaving a company before the vesting period is over may result in you losing some or all of the company's match, anything you put into your retirement account yourself will always belong to you.

For example, a resident in a three-year program who has a 3% match with an all-or-nothing vesting period of five years would need to work for the same company for an additional two years after residency before the 3% match would belong to him or her. Leaving the company at the end of residency would result in forfeiting the 3% match. However, the resident in this case would still own whatever he or she contributed his or her retirement account, no matter when they leave the company.

Alternatively, if the program above had a five-year vesting period where employees vested 20% per year, the resident could leave at the end of the three-year program with 60% of the matched contributions, plus everything that he or she contributed.

If your employer does offer a match, be sure to check if there is a vesting period to determine whether you would qualify for this benefit based on the length of your training program.

Types of Investments (Assets)

There are five common investments that residents are likely to consider purchasing:

- Stocks
- Bonds
- Mutual Funds
- Index Funds
- Target Date Funds

On the following pages, each of these investments is briefly described. The key differences in these investments are also outlined in Table 5.2.

Stocks

Stock in a company is a type of claim to the value of that company. In order to raise money, companies sell these claims in parts called shares. The more shares of a company's stock you own, the larger the share of the company's value to which you have a claim.

The price of a stock tends to fluctuate with the perceived value of the company (e.g., if the company's perceived value goes up, the stock price also tends to increase). Individual stocks are tied to the success or failure of a single company and are therefore viewed as highly risky investments; they could produce very high returns or deeply negative losses. If you plan to invest in individual stocks (Note: This is not at all recommended), diversifying your investments across many individual stocks is a way to reduce risk.

Table 5.2. Types of Investments/Assets (Groceries)

Investment Type	Risk[†]	Expected Return[†]	Cost	Recommended for Residents
Stocks (individual)	Higher	Variable	Very low	No
Bonds (individual)	Lower	Lower	Very low	No
Mutual Funds	Variable	Variable	Variable	Maybe
Index Funds	Variable	Variable	Very low	Yes*
Target Date Funds	Variable (age-matched)	Variable (age-matched)	Low	Yes*

[†] The risk and return characteristics listed are generalities only; they are not representative of all investments within a category. Some investments within a given category may stray from the generalities listed here.

* Index funds are a good option for residents who want to be relatively more involved in their investments over time. Target date funds are a good option for those who want minimal involvement.

Bonds

Bonds can be thought of as a type of loan where the investor is loaning money to the bond issuer. In return for this investment, the investor is promised to receive this same amount back at the end of a period of time in addition to interest payments along the way. The technical term for the amount the investor pays the issuer is the "par value" or "face value" of the bond; the interest payment from a bond is referred to as the "coupon rate." While there are spectrums of how risky and how rewarding different bond investments can be, bonds are generally considered lower-risk and lower-yield than stocks.

Mutual Funds

Mutual funds are "pooled investments" that generally contain stocks, bonds, or a mixed group of stocks and bonds. Investors in mutual funds buy shares of the *fund* (as opposed to shares of a single company), thereby gaining investment exposure to all the investments within the fund. Mutual funds are generally categorized by the goals of the fund. For example:

- A "growth" fund may contain higher-risk stocks with the goal of obtaining higher returns

- A "value" fund may contain stocks that fund managers believe are currently underpriced

- An "investment grade" bond fund may contain bonds from sources that are considered stable and reliable

Through holding many different individual investments in one place (a concept known as *diversification*), the risk associated with investing in mutual funds is generally considered to be much lower than the risk of investing in any of its component parts.

The intrinsic diversification of mutual funds is appealing; however, keeping these funds up to date and in compliance with regulations has costs. These costs are passed on to investors as fees, the most common of which is an *expense ratio*. Expense ratios can be thought of as the cost to own a portion of the fund; they are expressed as the percentage of your investment that goes to the fund managers each year (e.g., if you had $1,000 in a mutual fund with an expense ratio of 0.15%, $1.50 would be taken out to pay the fund managers each year). Guidelines for expense ratio limits are discussed later (see "Costs" on page 77).

Less common fees are "loads," which are costs associated with buying (*front-end load*) or selling (*back-end load*) funds. Care should be taken when selecting mutual funds to minimize these expenses, including avoiding any fund with any kind of load.

Index Funds

Index funds are also "pooled investments." Index funds can be thought of as a special type of mutual fund[32] where the goal of the fund is to match the performance of a certain benchmark (i.e., an "index"), such as the Standard and Poor's 500 (S&P 500) Index. This goal of tracking with an index is less complex than attempting to outperform an index, which is what many mutual funds try to do. Accordingly, index funds typically have lower expense ratios than traditional mutual funds.

Given their relatively low cost and broad diversification, total market index funds such as Vanguard's Total Stock Market Index Fund and Total Bond Market Index Fund have become popular investments. A popular investing strategy (the "three fund portfolio") even advocates for using only a few index funds for one's entire investment portfolio.[33]

Target Date Funds

Like mutual funds and index funds, target date funds are a third type of "pooled investment." Target date funds can be thought of as a special type of mutual fund[34] where the goal is to control and

---

[32] The actual structure of index funds a bit more complicated than this, but a detailed explanation of index fund structure is beyond the scope of this book.

[33] Larimore, T. (2018) *The Bogleheads' Guide to the Three-Fund Portfolio*. John Wiley & Sons, Inc.

[34] This is again a simplification. A detailed explanation of target date fund structure is beyond the scope of this book.

adjust the risk profile of the fund's investments as the target date (typically your retirement date) approaches. As you get closer to retirement, it usually makes sense to hold less risky investments (i.e., retirement is hopefully a time of preserving your wealth, not a time when you need to grow it).

The benefit of target date funds is that the risk profile of the pool of investments is automatically adjusted over time. While you are far from retirement and therefore have plenty of time to recover in case the market drops, target date funds will typically have a large proportion of riskier assets like stocks. As the years go by and you approach retirement, the target date fund managers adjust the ratio of investments from more risky to less risky.

This type of fund is highly recommended for those who do not want to be regularly involved in checking and adjusting their investments. Other names for this type of fund include "lifecycle," "dynamic-risk," or "age-based" funds.

Practical Applications

Which account (grocery bag) should I choose?

In general, if your employer offers a match, the answer is the employer-matched 401(k) or 403(b). Consider choosing the Roth option for this account if you have one available, and be sure to contribute enough to get the full match. If your employer does not offer a match, the best options are probably either a Roth IRA (assuming that you qualify) or unmatched contributions to your employer's retirement account—usually a 401(k) or 403(b), either Roth or traditional. Figure 5.2 outlines an algorithm to help decide which account to use for your investments during residency.

Note on Traditional IRAs

If your employer does not offer a 401(k) or 403(b) account for residents, it may be tempting to consider making pre-tax contributions to a traditional IRA that you set up yourself. While this seems reasonable, having pre-tax money in a traditional IRA will decrease the value of your ability to make "backdoor" Roth IRA contributions in the future. A full discussion of backdoor Roth IRAs is beyond the scope of this resource, so we will leave it at this: Try to avoid making pre-tax contributions to traditional IRAs. If your employer does not sponsor a 401(k) or 403(b), your best account option as a resident is likely a Roth IRA.

Figure 5.2. Investment account choice algorithm

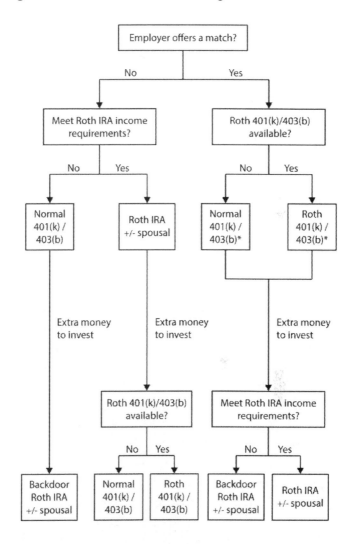

* At least up to the amount that your employer will match

Which assets (groceries) should I choose?

Answering this question completely involves determining your long-term financial goals, assessing your risk tolerance, and evaluating assets to find ones that match your goals and risk tolerance. In the interest of simplicity, we will abbreviate this discussion by assuming that residents are early in their career (i.e., many years from retirement), are seeking at least moderate returns, and are willing to accept a moderate amount of risk to pursue these returns.

If you don't want to worry about regularly checking in on your accounts and rebalancing your portfolio, buy a *target date fund* with the year in the name that is closest to your estimated year of retirement.

If you want to be more involved, your initial investment should likely be something with at least moderate projected returns (which usually comes with moderate risk). To this end, consider starting with a *US stock market index fund*. Note that with this approach (in contrast to using target date funds), you will be the one responsible for diversifying and rebalancing your assets to match your investment goals over time. Those that want to be more involved in their investments should read more than this book before creating their own investment plan. Consider starting with *The Boglehead's Guide to Investing.*[35]

Investing only in a total US stock market index fund while in residency is reasonable if it matches you risk tolerance and goals (consider using Vanguard's free asset allocation questionnaire[36] if you want help deciding how to distribute your investments based on personal factors). That said, most will

---

[35] Larimore, T., Lindauer, M., LeBoeuf, M. (2007) *The Boglehead's Guide to Investing.* Wiley.

[36] The Vanguard Group. (1995-2018) *Investor Questionnaire.* Retrieved from https://personal.vanguard.com/us/FundsInvQuestionnaire

probably find that they are interested in more diversification within a few years of graduation, if not immediately or later in training.

For those looking for more diversity in their portfolio while still only using index funds, one popular approach is the "three-fund portfolio." This concept and the next paragraph are only for those who are interested in significantly more involvement in their portfolios than the target date fund group. If you're happy with the target date fund strategy, feel free to skip to "Costs" below.

An entire book on the three-fund portfolio has recently been published,[37] but the short version is that owning (1) a total US stock market index fund, (2) a total international stock market index fund, and (3) a total US bond market index fund is a reasonable portfolio for most investors. Deciding how much goes into each of these funds is again a personal decision based on your goals and risk tolerance, but some loose guidance from the recent book on this topic is to own your age in bonds and the rest in stocks, 20% of which should go into the international stock market index fund.[24] For example, this would mean that a 30-year-old resident would have 30% of his or her investments in the US bond index fund, 14% in the international stock market index fund (20% of 70% = 14%), and 56% in the US stock market index fund. You can also use the Vanguard asset allocation questionnaire cited above to help with these decisions.

Costs

A key consideration when choosing between funds is cost; keeping costs low is a cornerstone of investing best practices.

---

[37] Larimore, T. (2018) *The Bogleheads' Guide to the Three-Fund Portfolio.* John Wiley & Sons, Inc.

Always look for accounts that are no-load (meaning you don't pay a commission just to put your money in or take it out) and have a low expense ratio (meaning you don't pay too much for fund management). Each of these costs will eat away at your returns, and they are collected even if your investments lose value. The assessment of large fees can be salt in the wounds of accounts that have already lost value. Minimizing the likelihood of this scenario requires keeping costs as low as possible.

In general, index funds should have expense ratios below 0.3% and target date funds should have expense ratios below 0.5%. Many traditional mutual funds will also have expense ratios less than 0.5%. Note that there are many options that have significantly lower expense ratios than those listed here. Choose the fund with the lowest costs that matches your desired level of risk, your goals, and the level of involvement you want to have in the routine management of your investments.

Expense Ratio Example Case

Resident A and Resident B both invest $10,000 into Roth 403(b) accounts. Resident A invests in Mutual Fund A, which has a 0.5% expense ratio. Resident B invests in Mutual Fund B, which has a 0.1% expense ratio. Both Mutual Fund A and Mutual Fund B grow 5% over the next 30 years.

How much does each resident have in his or her account after 30 years?

Resident A's return during that time will be 4.5% (5.0% return minus the 0.5% expense ratio). Resident B's return will be 4.9% (5.0% return minus the 0.1% expense ratio). This means that after 30 years, Resident A will have $4,548 less in his or her Roth 403(b) account than Resident B ($37,453 for Resident A vs. $42,001 for Resident B). This difference would be even greater if larger amounts of money were invested at these rates.

Summary

Should I be investing during residency?

If you (1) don't have any student loans, (2) have only low-interest (less than 4%) student loans, or (3) are pursuing Public Service Loan Forgiveness, then answer is probably yes. If you do have student loans—particularly if they are high-interest loans—and you are *not* pursuing Public Service Loan Forgiveness, the answer is more likely to be no, assuming you use leftover money to make extra payments on your loans instead.

The language of investing

Investments can be held in different types of accounts. The type of account determines how the investment is taxed. The most relevant types of accounts for residents are Roth IRA accounts, where you pay tax now and avoid tax later (which is good if you expect your income to go up in the future), and 401(k)/403(b) accounts, where you typically avoid tax now but pay tax later.[38] The most relevant investments for residents are index funds (large collections of individual investments that aim to follow an index, such as the total US stock market) and target date funds (large collections of individual investments that are automatically adjusted over time to decrease risk as you get closer to retirement). Index funds and target date funds are the most relevant investments for residents because they are *diversified* (i.e., they contain many different investments, which helps mitigate risk) and they are usually *low-cost* (i.e., the fees

---

[38] Some employers offer Roth 401(k)/403(b) accounts, where contributions are taxed going in but grow and can be withdrawn tax-free, similar to a Roth IRA.

associated with buying, maintaining, and selling these types of investments tend to be low).

Practical applications

An algorithm to help residents decide which initial investment account to choose is provided on page 75. Simple and reasonable investment options for residents include a total US stock market index fund or a target date fund (the one with the year closest to your anticipated retirement year in the name).

Action Items

☐ Decide if you should be investing during residency based on your budget, your financial goals, and your debt circumstances. If deciding to invest, continue with the steps below.

☐ Decide which type of investment account to open and open it.

☐ Decide which type of investments you would like to purchase (e.g., target date funds, index funds).

☐ Add money to your investment account.

☐ Purchase investments with the money in your account.

Chapter 6

Financial Advisors

Michael Ernst, MD and Eric Shappell, MD, MHPE

When considering hiring a financial advisor in residency, there are five questions that can help you navigate this decision:

Question #1
> *Should I hire a financial advisor in residency?*

Question #2
> *What credentials should I look for in a financial advisor?*

Question #3
> *How are financial advisors paid?*

Question #4
> *How much will a financial advisor cost?*

Question #5
> *Where can I find a financial advisor?*

Should I Hire a Financial Advisor in Residency?

Most residents should be able to get along just fine with only a few hours dedicated to researching the basic financial decisions of residency: (1) choosing a loan repayment plan, (2) choosing which insurance products to purchase and when, and (3) what to do with any extra income (typically a decision of whether to make extra payments on loans vs. invest). If you don't feel comfortable making these decisions on your own and aren't interested in learning more about them yourself, choosing to hire a financial advisor may be the way to go. This also may be a good idea if you have unusually complex financial circumstances.

What Credentials Should I Look for in a Financial Advisor?

Unlike the title of "resident physician," which we all associate with a relatively homogeneous educational and experiential background (e.g., medical school didactics, clerkships, etc.), the term "financial advisor" is far more general and can be used to describe anyone—regardless of their educational or experiential background—who provides financial advice to customers. Examples of other titles that may be held by "financial advisors" include:

- Financial Planner / Consultant / Specialist
- Investment Adviser
- Accountant
- Insurance Agent
- Registered representative (a.k.a. "Broker")

As you might expect from all these different titles, not all "financial advisors" have the same level of knowledge and/or experience, nor do they all offer the same services. Some are guaranteed to be salespeople (e.g., insurance agents, brokers) while others may not sell anything other than their advice. For these reasons, it is important to familiarize yourself with some distinctions that can help you understand different advisors' credentials. In Table 6.1, we highlight distinctions that convey a certain level of personal finance knowledge and/or experience.

For residents looking for someone with personal finance knowledge and experience to help them create a financial plan, consider an advisor with a Certified Financial Planner (CFP), Chartered Financial Consultant (ChFC), or Certified Public Accountant / Personal Finance Specialist (CPA/PFS) designation. Most residents don't have large investment accounts or nuanced investing strategies that would warrant an investment specialist such as a Chartered Financial Analyst (CFA).

Table 6.1. Titles for professionals offering personal finance advice

Title	Abbr.	Focus	Notes
"Financial Planner" "Financial Advisor" "Financial Consultant" "Investment Consultant"	N/A	N/A	No regulations limit those who can refer to themselves using these titles These titles are for marketing purposes; they convey no meaningful information about knowledge or experience
Certified Financial Planner	CFP	General Personal Finance	Most widely recognized credential for financial advisors Similar to ChFC
Chartered Financial Consultant	ChFC	General Personal Finance	Similar to CFP
Certified Public Accountant / Personal Financial Specialist	CPA / PFS	CPA: Taxes PFS: General Personal Finance	For those already holding a Certified Public Accountant (CPA) title, the Personal Finance Specialist (PFS) designation can be obtained by completing an additional exam
Chartered Financial Analyst	CFA	Investing	Degree designed to signify expertise in investing—does not require general personal finance knowledge or experience

Note: Those interested in a deep dive into financial credentials and/or looking up other credentials for a prospective financial advisor can do so on the Financial Industry Regulatory Authority (FINRA) website.[39] Abbr. = abbreviation.

---

[39] Financial Industry Regulatory Authority. (2018) *Professional Designations*. Retrieved from http://www.finra.org/investors/professional-designations

How Are Financial Advisors Paid?

There are several potential revenue streams for financial advisors, including:

- Commissions
- Percentage of assets under management (AUM)
- Retainer fees
- Hourly rates
- Flat fees

These types of payments are not mutually exclusive. For example, an advisor may both charge an hourly rate and collect commissions on the products they sell. Be careful to clarify all of the revenue streams leading to a potential financial advisor before you consider hiring one, since certain types of revenue streams can result in bias.

Commissions

It has been well established that doctors with financial conflicts of interest (e.g., from the pharmaceutical industry) exhibit biases in their practices. Commissions are a form of financial conflict of interest for advisors; accordingly, advisors who sell products for which they receive commissions are at high risk of exhibiting biases in their advice to you. If your advisor is paid commissions, you may be talked into buying a product that makes the advisor more money, rather than the one that is best for you. For this reason, we recommend keeping your advice and your purchases separate. Ask any potential financial advisors if they are paid on commissions; if they are, consider a different advisor.

Percentage of Assets Under Management

Advisors who are paid a percentage of assets under management (AUM) take a cut of the total amount of money that they manage for you. While in this model the investment incentives of the advisor align with yours (i.e., the more they grow your portfolio, the more valuable their cut becomes), there are many problems with this model, several of which are detailed in the following paragraphs.

First, most advisors who use an AUM payment structure require clients to have a minimum amount of money to be managed (thus ensuring a minimum amount of their cut). Most residents with small or non-existent investment accounts will not meet these minimum amounts and thus won't qualify for their services.

A second problem with this model occurs on the other end of the spectrum, when you have a large amount of money invested. In this case, the cut that you end up paying the advisor can become very large and is very unlikely to be worth the cost (e.g., an AUM fee of 1% on a $3 million portfolio is $30,000 – do you really think your advisor is adding $30,000 of value to that portfolio every year?).

Finally, while the advisor will make more money if your portfolio grows faster by getting better returns, this doesn't mean that AUM advisors are dedicating all of their time to make sure they get you every last bit of return they can. Consider this: An AUM advisor's return on obtaining a new client with the same portfolio size as you is 100 times greater than his or her return on getting you another 1% out of your portfolio (i.e., 1% of a new client's $1,000,000 portfolio would be $10,000, whereas making you another 1% on your portfolio would only increase his or her cut by $100, which is 1% of the extra 1% he or she made you on your $1,000,000 portfolio). How would you spend your time if the yield on one project was 100 times that of another?

In summary, sure, the investment interests of AUM advisors do align with those of their clients, but the degree and significance of this alignment is easy to overestimate.

Retainer Fee

Retainer fees are payments made at a regular interval for a set of financial services. When used exclusively, this arrangement can be used to avoid the conflicts of interest that come with commissions and the runaway costs that come with the AUM fee structure. In spite of these benefits, residents are unlikely to have financial circumstances changing rapidly enough to warrant having someone on retainer. It is much more likely that residents seeking financial advice just need a one-time roadmap and a point in the right direction.

Hourly Rate / Flat Fee

An hourly rate or flat fee structure will be appropriate for most residents. There are a limited number of financial decisions that need to be made during training (e.g., strategies for loan repayment, insurance, and investing); once a strategy for approaching each of these issues has been established, it is unlikely that residents will require additional advice. For this reason, a one-time meeting with an hourly or flat fee advisor is likely the most appropriate and cost-effective way for residents to obtain professional financial advice.

Other Terms

<u>Fee-Only</u>

Advisors described as fee-*only* are only paid by you (i.e., they are not paid commissions by outside companies for selling you products). Fee-only advisors can be hourly, a flat fee, a retainer fee, or a percentage of AUM.

<u>Fee-Based</u>

Advisors who are fee-*based* may collect reimbursements from other sources, including commissions on products they sell you, in addition to the fee(s) that they charge you directly. As discussed previously in the context of commissions, this outside revenue stream causes a conflict of interest and can lead to biased advice. Be sure to clarify how prospective advisors are paid to make sure you understand the full cost and any potential biases associated with their services.

Fee-only vs. Fee-based

Note the important distinction between these payment schedules:

- *Fee-only* advisors are only paid by you
- *Fee-based* advisors get paid by you *and* may receive reimbursement from outside sources, such as commissions for selling you certain financial products

Since there is a conflict of interest that comes with the commissions of fee-based advice, fee-only advisors are generally preferable to fee-based advisors.

How Much Will a Financial Advisor Cost?

The fees associated with financial advice vary widely based on factors such as services offered, credentials, experience, and geography. Some approximate rates and fee schedules for financial advisors are listed in Table 6.2.

Table 6.2. Approximate costs for financial advisors by type

Type	Cost
Hourly rate	$100 - $250 per hour
Flat fee	$500 - $3,000
Retainer fee	$2,000 - $10,000 per year
Percentage of AUM	0.25-2.0% of entire portfolio
Fee-based	Variable fee *plus* commissions

Where Can I Find a Financial Advisor?

Financial advisors can be independent agents or part of a larger firm. A great place to find an advisor is through the National Association of Personal Finance Advisors (NAPFA), an organization of fee-only advisors. You can search for local fee-only advisors on the NAPFA website.[40] Note that some advisors on this site charge AUM fees, not just flat fees or hourly rates.

---

[40] The National Association of Personal Finance Advisors. (2018) Retrieved from https://www.napfa.org/

Summary

Should I hire a financial advisor in residency?

In spite of how it may feel, the financial situations of most residents just aren't that complicated. If you're willing to spend a few hours learning the absolute basics of personal finance, chances are you'll be fine without one. If you're a novice and completely uninterested in learning more about personal finance, you might want to pay for some help.

What credentials should I look for in a financial advisor?

Look for someone with a CFP (Certified Financial Planner), ChFC (Chartered Financial Consultant), or CPA/PFS (Certified Public Accountant / Personal Financial Specialist) designation.

How are financial advisors paid?

By one or more of the following: flat, recurring, or hourly fees, taking a percentage of your portfolio (also call "assets under management" or AUM), or commissions on what he or she sells you. For residents, we believe that advisors with flat fees or hourly rates will usually be the most appropriate and cost-effective way for residents to obtain professional financial advice.

How much will a financial advisor cost?

For the type of advisor we prefer (i.e., flat or hourly fee-only), somewhere around $500-1,000 for a flat fee or $100-250 per hour.

Where can I find a financial advisor?

Check out the National Association of Personal Finance Advisors (NAPFA) website.[41] NAPFA is an organization of fee-only financial advisors. Note that some advisors on this site charge AUM fees, not just flat fees or hourly rates.

Action Items

☐ Decide if you need professional help with your upcoming financial decisions. If you decide that you do, continue through the steps below.

☐ Make a list of specific questions you have for the financial advisor.

☐ Make a list of potential fee-only financial advisors based on colleague recommendations and/or an online search.

☐ Hire your financial advisor after researching and, if you would like, interviewing the advisors on your list.

---

[41] The National Association of Personal Finance Advisors. (2018) Retrieved from https://www.napfa.org/

Chapter 7

Pearls and Pitfalls

Eric Shappell, MD, MHPE

There are several important points on resident finances that don't fit cleanly into one of the previous chapters. In this chapter, we've gathered a number of these common financial pearls and pitfalls that residents are likely to encounter during training.

People who say "you won't have any money in residency" are wrong.

It is common for residents to believe that they will spend their entire paycheck on living expenses and have nothing left for savings, retirement, or insurance products. This is not true.

How much money you have to put toward growing and protecting your wealth in residency depends on how you budget. Most residents who are deliberate in limiting their spending will have some funds left over to use for these purposes.

Have a plan for where your extra funds will go (in order).

Between paying down debt, saving for retirement, and building up an emergency fund, there are usually plenty of worthwhile places to put extra funds as a resident. The problem many residents have is deciding, out of all these great places to direct your funds, where should they go? As with most things in personal finance, there is no "correct" answer; you must make an informed choice based on your options and personal priorities.

Here is one approach that you can use as a starting point:

1. Emergency fund (up to your goal amount)
2. High interest debt (>8%)
3. Student loans[42] *or* investing[43]
4. Whichever option you didn't choose in #3

With most student loan balances measured in hundreds of thousands and at least $24,000 per year usually available in tax-advantaged retirement accounts,[44] few and far between will be the residents who get past step three, and getting past step four will in most cases require another source of income (e.g., a working spouse). If you are fortunate enough to be in the small group of people that maxes out each of these options and still has extra funds left over while still in training (residents without debt or pursuing PSLF are more likely to fall into this category), there

---

[42] Remember that, if pursuing PSLF, making extra student loan payments will decrease the value you can potentially get from the program. For a list of factors to consider when deciding whether to pay down student loans or invest, see page 61.

[43] For an algorithm to help decide which retirement account to choose, see page 75. Don't forget about spousal accounts when investing.

[44] This calculation is based on 2018 tax limits: $18,500 in 401(k)/403(b) + $5,500 in Roth IRA = $24,000.

are many different directions you could go after these four steps (e.g., saving up for a down payment on a house, saving for college for your children, or investing in a taxable account). Since so few residents will fall into this category, discussion of next steps after the four listed above is beyond the scope of this book.

What you can afford is more a matter of your priorities than your income.

Just because you have $250 left over from each paycheck after paying for essentials does not mean you can afford a new watch every month. If your priority is to grow your wealth as much as possible during residency, that $250 belongs in a retirement account or contributed toward paying down debt.

In your budget, you should set the amount you will allow yourself to spend (i.e., what you can "afford") in each financial category (e.g., rent, insurance, savings, discretionary spending). The decision of where to set your spending limit in each category should be deliberate and reflect your priorities. If there are times you find yourself with funds left over, they should be contributed to the category you prioritize the most—not defaulted into discretionary spending.

Spending too much on housing will destroy your budget.

Residents too often allow costs to expand in their budget like gases expanding to the size of their container. This can be particularly damaging if it happens with housing, since it is often the largest expense in a resident's budget and it is tough to fix— mainly because you'll have a lease or mortgage agreement to deal with before you can move to a cheaper place. Housing has the potential to destroy your financial flexibility before you even realize it was there.

When planning your housing while in residency, carefully consider your priorities and the full spectrum of options available (including roommates). For most residents, every piece of the budget puzzle will be smaller than housing; accordingly, this factor that has the greatest potential impact on your cash flow— negative or positive.

Owning a home has downsides.

For some reason, many residents are in a big hurry to own a home. Overestimating the benefits of owning and failing to account for the benefits of renting creates a false notion that paying rent is "throwing away money" and that owning a home is "building wealth." A full discussion of this topic is beyond the scope of this book; however, we will highlight a few key points here. Those interested in further discussion on this topic can find more in-depth resources online.[45]

Two key reasons that residents who are considering buying a home should proceed with extreme caution are:

- Your mortgage is the *minimum* you will spend on housing, whereas rent is a *maximum*.

    If a pipe bursts in the home you own, it's your time, money, and energy that need to be spent to fix it. Hopefully you'll have enough money in your emergency fund to cover it. If a pipe bursts in the apartment you rent, it's the landlord's problem.

---

[45] The White Coat Investor. (2018) *10 Reasons Why Residents Shouldn't Buy a House*. Retrieved from https://www.whitecoatinvestor.com/10-reasons-why-residents-shouldnt-buy-a-house

- Mortgage payments only count as "building wealth" once you account for transaction costs and the change in value of the home.

    Buying and selling a home is expensive. Your wealth will take a hit when you pay the fees required to buy the home, and it will likely take another hit when you pay the fees necessary to sell it. For you to walk away with a greater net worth than when you started, the monetary benefits of owning the home (i.e., appreciation, mostly) need to overcome the costs. It's not as simple as "mortgage payment = wealth building." Residents with short training periods should be particularly careful when considering buying a home while in training. A "rent vs. buy" calculator such as the one provided by the New York Times[46] can also be useful in comparing housing options, particularly to account for the hidden costs of things like property taxes and association fees.

Investing is not supposed to be "fun."

You might find investing to be satisfying, fulfilling, or even rewarding; however, if investing feels "fun," or if you are looking for short-term gains, you need to be careful. There's a fine line between investing and gambling, and you don't want to be gambling with your retirement.

We concede that it can be exciting to open up your first account, select which investment(s) will be in your starting portfolio, and contribute your first round of funding. After the

---

[46] Bostock, M., Carter, S., Tse, A. (2018) Is It Better to Rent or Buy? Retrieved from https://www.nytimes.com/interactive/2014/upshot/buy-rent-calculator.html

initial planning and implementation, however, good investing tends to be a matter of simply staying the course (something that few people would describe as "fun").

While it is considered good practice to occasionally check your account to make sure your investments still have the breakdown you want (a practice called "rebalancing" your portfolio; for example, checking whether your stock index fund still makes up 80% of your portfolio and your bond market index fund makes up 20% and adjusting if necessary), the temptation to frequently check investments should generally be resisted— particularly if you're opening up your account dashboard looking for "fun."

Behavior can be more important than knowledge.

Armed with only a rudimentary understanding of personal finance, the disciplined resident can outperform even the savviest resident investor, assuming that resident is not also disciplined. Think of it this way: If you can't bring yourself to carve money out of your budget each month to put towards student loans or retirement savings, then it doesn't matter what the returns on your investments would be. You need to save money before you can get your foot in the door with investing. For this reason, practicing good saving habits should be an early priority. Once these habits are established, the focus can shift to optimizing investment returns.

Conclusion

We hope that this book has increased your financial knowledge, inspired you to set financial goals, and given you the information you need to see your goals through.

While some will take what they have learned, apply it to their financial circumstances, and move on with their lives, we hope that others will finish this book with a hunger for more. Fortunately, there is a wealth of personal finance content available online and in print. We encourage those looking for other personal finance books and resources to visit the recommended reading section of the MD in the Black website.[47] On this page you will find links to the best personal finance content we find, both in print and from around the web.

In addition to recommended reading, we have also dedicated a page on the MD in the Black website to clarifications

---

[47] MD in the Black. (2018) *Recommended Reading*. Retrieved from https://www.MDintheBlack.com/recommended-reading

and corrections of the content in this book.[48] Our top priority is making sure that you have the information you need to make reasonable and informed financial decisions while in training, so if you find something in this book to be complicated, confusing, or incorrect, please reach out to us at MDintheBlack@gmail.com and we will post a response on this page addressing the issue. We encourage you to visit this page even if you don't submit feedback to make sure you are aware of any needed corrections or clarifications that were identified by others.

---

[48] MD in the Black. (2018) *Errata*. Retrieved from
https://www.MDintheBlack.com/errata

MD in the Black

Contact

We want to hear from you!

Whether it's feedback on this book, questions about our curriculum, or interest in collaborating on research projects, we're excited to talk with you. Feel free to reach out to us any time, either by email or on twitter:

Email: MDintheBlack@gmail.com
Twitter: @MDintheBlack

We will also continue to update the MD in the Black website with new content, corrections, and commentary from our readers. Come visit us online:

www.MDintheBlack.com

29357322R00068

Made in the USA
Middletown, DE
21 December 2018